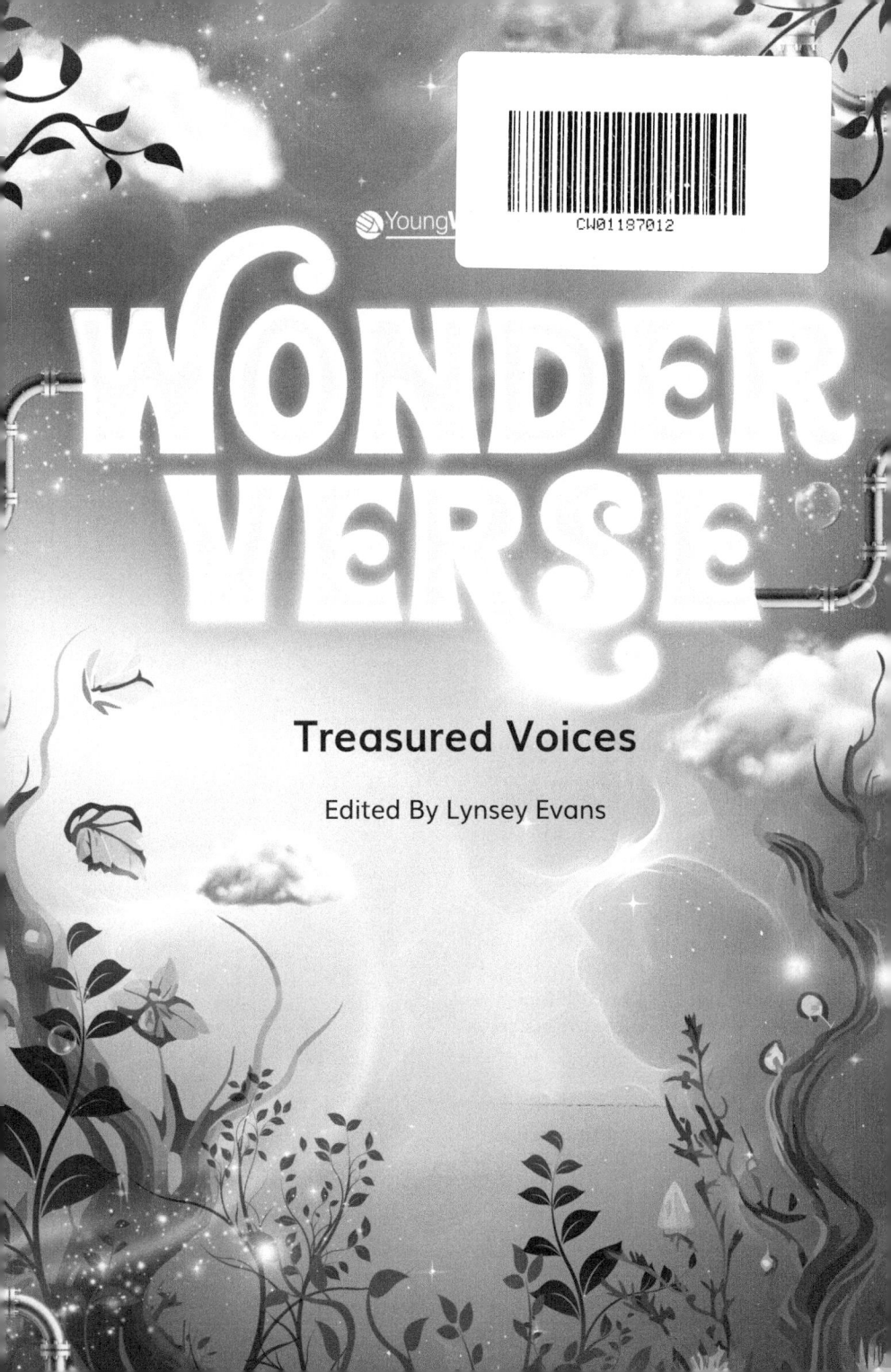

WONDER VERSE

Treasured Voices

Edited By Lynsey Evans

First published in Great Britain in 2025 by:

Young Writers
Remus House
Coltsfoot Drive
Peterborough
PE2 9BF
Telephone: 01733 890066
Website: www.youngwriters.co.uk

All Rights Reserved
Book Design by Ashley Janson
© Copyright Contributors 2024
Softback ISBN 978-1-83685-138-7
Printed and bound in the UK by BookPrintingUK
Website: www.bookprintinguk.com
YB0624L

FOREWORD

WELCOME READER,

For Young Writers' latest competition *Wonderverse*, we asked primary school pupils to explore their creativity and write a poem on any topic that inspired them. They rose to the challenge magnificently with some going even further and writing stories too! The result is this fantastic collection of writing in a variety of styles.

Here at Young Writers our aim is to encourage creativity in children and to inspire a love of the written word, so it's great to get such an amazing response, with some absolutely fantastic pieces. This open theme of this competition allowed them to write freely about something they are interested in, which we know helps to engage kids and get them writing. Within these pages you'll find a variety of topics, from hopes, fears and dreams, to favourite things and worlds of imagination. The result is a collection of brilliant writing that showcases the creativity and writing ability of the next generation.

I'd like to congratulate all the young writers in this anthology, I hope this inspires them to continue with their creative writing.

CONTENTS

Anthony Roper Primary School, Eynsford

Julia Godfrey (8)	1
Amelia Webb (10)	2
Emily Jackson (9)	4
Axel Prahl Sorensen (7)	5
William Muckle (7)	6
Isla Glock (10)	7
Evie Voce (8)	8
Rosie Williams (8)	9
Scarlett Clay (7)	10
Belle Elliott (8)	11
Evelyn Carter (8)	12
Poppy O'Neill (9)	13
Talula Purcell (8)	14
Thomas McMillan (7)	15

Barton Moss Community Primary School, Eccles

Santannamae Smith (7)	16
Logan Birkett (7)	17
Yousef Alkeshif (9)	18
Joseph William (7)	19
Logan Bell (7)	20
Poppy Farley Kirby (9)	21
Inioluwa Falusi (7)	22
Jacob Taylor (9)	23
Joseph Dean (8)	24
Sophia Rosewhite (7)	25
Christopher Oxton (7)	26
Imogen Taylor (7)	27
Tiwatope Daniel (8)	28
Greyson Atherton (7)	29
Connor Swanson (7)	30

Henry Willetts (10)	31
Evie-Leigh Evans (7)	32
Melissa da Silva Bavaroski (10)	33
Charlie McCarthy Boyle (11)	34
Max Appleton (10)	35
Dakota Baker (11)	36
Lylah Wells (10)	37
Sonny Macdonald-Boyd (10)	38
Clara Swanson (10)	39
Jayden Sufyaan (10)	40
Dillon Shannon-Larkin (10)	41
Chloe Griffiths (10)	42
Abimael Remesha (10)	43
Lindsay Umbaca (10)	44
George Firth (10)	45
Krystal Wynter (11)	46
Scarlett Gilbert (10)	47

Blythefield Primary School, Belfast

Lucia Sullivan (9)	48
Hilton Gorman (9)	49
Amelia Rea (10)	50
Kayleb Wightman (10)	51

Fawcett Primary School, Trumpington

Zoë Appleyard (9)	52
Lewis Jack Chesters (9)	54
Akira Lyons (9)	55
Lucy Zhang (9)	56
River Szabo (9)	57
Lena Nikolic (9)	58

Greenways Primary Academy, Stockton Brook

Emmie Mae Dalzell (9)	59
Jack Stokes (9)	60
Myra Kumar (10)	61

Kingsbury Primary School, Tamworth

Millie-Rae Francis (10)	62
Georgia Addison (9)	64
Jasmine (10)	65
Philippa Harrison (10)	66
Evelyn Stokes (9)	67
Jessica Hawkins (10)	68
Summer-Marie Mari Dockerill (9)	69
Scarlett Pardoe (10)	70
Caiden-Jay Price-Butler (9)	71
Ali-James Djenad (10)	72
Layla Carnell (10)	73
Jacob Blackwell (9)	74
George Abbott (10)	75
Shelbie (10)	76
Emmy Baker (9)	77
Eddie (9)	78
Evie Hope (10)	79
Alfie De Paola (11)	80
Felicity Green (10)	81
Myah Patel (9)	82
Ruby Benton (10)	83
Harley (9)	84
Elin (9)	85
Georgie Brooks (10)	86
Bradley Swan (9)	87
Lacey Carruthers (9)	88
Lola Robinson-Stanley (10)	89
Amelia Dunn (9)	90
Freddie Vaughan (9)	91
Tyler (10)	92
Isaac Maloney (9)	93
James Charlton (10)	94
Alfie Barnett (9)	95
Sofia (10)	96

Rueben (11)	97
Harvey Baker-Lewis (10)	98
Isabella (10)	99
Billy Kinsey (10)	100
Kate (10)	101
Sophia Henson (10)	102
Alice (10)	103
Darcy-May Hollingsworth (10)	104
Roxy Dovey (11)	105
Jack Stewart (11)	106
Bradley Smith (11)	107
Olivia Holland (11)	108
Millie (10)	109
Bella (10)	110
Ava (9)	111
Mikey K-S (10)	112
Connor Brunn (11)	113
Poppy Dowdall Ford (10)	114
Erin	115
Riley B (10)	116
Annie (10)	117
Chloe Spooner (11)	118
Scarlett (9)	119
Izaiyah Ashton (9)	120

Oakridge Junior School, Basingstoke

Jiya Palikondawar (9)	121
Avana Rai (8)	122
Samuel July (10)	123
Ankush Dhara (9)	124
Harris Snyder (8)	125
Tarunya Yakeshwaran (9)	126
Namaya Whitby (7)	127
Gabriel Daniel (9)	128
Greatness John (9)	129
Cami Durham (10)	130
Daisy Pocock (9)	131
Dunamis John (7)	132
Jasmine Jelf (7) & Freya	133

Rushton Primary School, Rushton

Elula Manning (11)	134
Sophia Holland (10)	136
Elsa Monk (10)	137
Lawrie Adams-Knowles (11)	138
Amelia Scott (11)	139
Jaya Pooni (10)	140
Sophia Burnside (10)	141
Martha Ambery (11)	142

St Jerome CE Bilingual School, Harrow

Elyas Ladak (11)	143
Eliana Dotse (10)	144
Aaradhya Butani (10)	146
Evangeline Penhale (9)	148
Antonia Radu (10)	149
Pranshu Patel (9)	150
Esther Afari (10)	151
Katalea Lusha (10)	152
Chloe Giorgi (10)	153
Bronwen Taylor (9)	154
Zain Elfara (10)	155
Eloise Kira Misra (8)	156
Clayton Taylor (9)	157
Huda Alinzi (9)	158
Sara Jang (9)	159
Georgie Gilbert Farnan (9)	160
Zuzanna Pasternak (9)	161
Vinicius Tonelli Alves (9)	162
Sima Alkam (10)	163
Phoebe Afzal (9)	164
Ayra Gupta (9)	165
Alessia Zgripcea (10)	166
Advik Dubey (7)	167
Zaynah Abdirizak (9)	168
Lily Morsley (10)	169
Vidhan Patel (9)	170
Bethany Olewe (11)	171
Akrish Singh (9)	172
Hannah Elisabeth Lopez Rohrmueller (9)	173
Aksh Patel (9)	174
David Oliveira (10)	175
Avika Gupta (10)	176
Caspian Nunn (9)	177
Asher Wellington (10)	178
Jana Alhilal (10)	179
Antoni Plantowski (9)	180

St Osmund's CE Middle School, Dorchester

Tommy Richardson (11)	181
Mya Thorne (10)	182
Louisa Graham (11)	184
Imogen Spracklen (10)	186
Esmaya Richards (10)	187
Temiloluwa Adenigba (9)	188
Annabelle Biswell Harvey (10)	189
Molly Hurford (10)	190
Lilly Warren (10)	191
Poppy Norman (9)	192

St Therese's Catholic Primary School, Sandsfields

Niamh Lewis (10)	193
Sarena Hanford (10)	194
Arabella Lowe (10)	195
Cameron O'Mahony (10)	196
Noah Gibbs (10)	197
Dorothea Boland (11)	198
West Mainwaring (10)	199
Camden Greenwood (10)	200

Seasons

Spring, the season of rebirth and renewal,
As the world awakens from winter's funeral.
Flowers bloom and the trees come alive,
As nature's beauty, once again, we revive.

Summer, the season of warmth and light,
As the sun shines down with all its might.
Beaches, barbecues and lazy days,
As we revel in the sun's fiery blaze.

Fall, the season of change and transition,
As leaves turn and the colours glisten.
The air turns crisp and the nights grow long,
As we prepare for winter's chill and its song.

Winter, the season of cold and snow,
As the world becomes a white, icy glow.
Frost on the windows and snow on the ground,
As we huddle up and winter's joys are found.

Each season, with its own unique grace,
A cycle of life that we all embrace.
The beauty of nature forever will it last,
As they witness the seasons of the present and the past.

Julia Godfrey (8)
Anthony Roper Primary School, Eynsford

Best Friends But Not Related

We may not share a name or blood
That matters not to me
I could not love you more
If you were family

You recognise my differences and fears
But never stop to judge me
And whenever we disagree
You never hold a grudge

You've seen me through the worst of times
And helped my heart heal
You lift me up when I am down
And care for how I feel

Sometimes we catch each other's eye
And know the other's thoughts
And other times we laugh so hard
My stomach is in knots

It brings me joy that we can talk
For hours on end
We have a beautiful connection
And I am glad to call you my best friends

So know, we are not family
But you still make my heart whole
Even though we are not blood-related
We will always be sisters at heart.

Amelia Webb (10)
Anthony Roper Primary School, Eynsford

My Autumn

A utumn - use your senses to listen to the leaves crunch, feel the bumps on the logs and trees, smell your neighbour's pumpkin cake, taste the fruit you have picked and tell me how it tastes, look at the leaves falling and make some art.
U nder the trees can you spot the fairies where they twinkle and twirl and where they grant your wishes?
T ell spooky stories around the campfire and eat marshmallows.
U sually I stay inside and do art, but in autumn I go into the woods and get leaves to do art.
M ake your Halloween costume. Don't go out and buy one every year, just make one, it's something to do.
N arrate everything in a notebook and then make a poem out of it, just like me.

Emily Jackson (9)
Anthony Roper Primary School, Eynsford

Dug's And Nug's Day

I know a dog, his name is Dug
He has big brown eyes and two floppy ears
A wrinkly head and a sad little mug
You have guessed, Dug is a Pug
Dug has a brother who looks the same
Except he's brown and his name is Nug
They go to the park where they see their friends
Goldie the Golden Retriever, a Dalmatian called Ben
Jackie the Jack Russell, and his brother Len
They like to play catch and they like to play tug of war
They like to dig holes and they like to chase bugs
They go for a swim and chase the fish
Wishing they'll catch some for their dinner dish
When they wear out their little feet
They go home for something to eat
A fish in a dish, a snuggle on a rug,
That's a day in the life of Dug and Nug!

Axel Prahl Sorensen (7)
Anthony Roper Primary School, Eynsford

My Trip To The Zoo

Look at the panda, look at its paws,
Look at the tiger, hear how it roars.
Look at the giraffe and its long, long neck,
Look at the parrot peck, peck, peck.
Look at the monkeys, all different types,
Look at the polar bear, all snowy and white.
Look at the chameleon, just the right colour,
Look at the rhino raging like thunder.
Look at the zebras making an illusion,
Look at the wildebeest in confusion.
Look at the hyenas, hear them laugh,
Look at the elephants taking a bath.
So many things to see at the zoo,
I love it, how about you?

William Muckle (7)
Anthony Roper Primary School, Eynsford

Friends

From the day life starts until it ends
We have the chance to make lots of friends.
They chatted all about lifeline
To chatter to pass the time.
To show support to be your friend
You try so hard but too hard
They don't like you.
Mean has four letters, but so does kind.
You always have a better side.
You always have a choice, so choose the better side.
As life goes on, you get friends and lose friends
Even though you lose friends
You can get them back
If you get in a fight - say sorry.
If they don't like you
Then let them try to like you.

Isla Glock (10)
Anthony Roper Primary School, Eynsford

Stormy Sea

The stormy sea is full of fierce waves,
As the violent lightning strikes against the rocks,
Fiercely the thunder gasps at the rainy clouds,
The dancing seaweed is hoping for a
Great ten out of ten from the uncontrolled fish,
Silent secrets hide between the broken shipwrecks,
Foamy froth is growing as time runs by,
The clouds over-run the dark night sky,
Fish are jumping out of the relentless waves,
Galloping waves are pounding the shoreline,
Roaring thunder shouts at the striking lightning,
Waves look over the angry sea.

Evie Voce (8)
Anthony Roper Primary School, Eynsford

Seasons Change

Nature changes in different ways,
You will see it every day.
Everywhere it grows, oxygen flows.
Colourful leaves and conkers fall in autumn,
While winter snow brings joy to all.
The spring glow helps the plants to grow,
As raindrops fall, it helps the flowers we sow.
When summer comes around,
And the sun shines down,
On the people on the ground.
The evenings last longer,
Until the blazing sun goes down,
And then the bright moon will appear
And take its place in the sunset.

Rosie Williams (8)
Anthony Roper Primary School, Eynsford

My Friends

Friends are fun, friends are great.
Friends are there for us to appreciate.
From high to low.
From small until we grow.
Friends are forever.
I feel best when we are together.
This is my poem for my friends
Who bring me laughter and happiness that never ends.
Small friends and tall friends from every religion.
I cannot think of a better vision.
Playing, dancing and having the most fun.
I can honestly say friendships are the one.

Scarlett Clay (7)
Anthony Roper Primary School, Eynsford

Seasons

In spring the daffodils open, the tulips dance and the lambs are woken.

In summer the evenings are lighter, I play with my friends because the sun shines brighter.

In autumn the leaves are falling, pumpkins need picking and Halloween's calling.

In winter the snowflakes are falling and Santa is calling, "Naughty or nice?"

Another year's finished, we love the ice.

Belle Elliott (8)
Anthony Roper Primary School, Eynsford

Coming Home

The ocean is jumping against the rocks and waves lick away footsteps in the sand.
The rain is coming down to meet the sea and the stars are playing hide-and-seek with the clouds.
The thunder grumbles like a little bear, while the lightning silently screams towards the ground.
Waves play with each other like Jack Russells, as they carry the boat towards the shore and home.

Evelyn Carter (8)
Anthony Roper Primary School, Eynsford

The Sights And Sounds Of Autumn

Seasons change
Leaves change
Big bonfires
Little mittens
Crackling, crunchy, orange leaves
Little robins singing their melodies
Magnificent horse chestnut trees dropping maroon conkers
Squirrels munch on their nuts
Orange pumpkins, some with warts and some with faces
Behaved bats ready to hibernate
Hedgehogs burrowing, ready to sleep.

Poppy O'Neill (9)
Anthony Roper Primary School, Eynsford

A Very Sunny Day

The ocean is just like a dog,
Dangerous in a way,
Always wants to jump and play,
Let the ocean sway in its own way,
What a lovely day,
Happy enough to make me say hooray,
What a sunny day,
Lying happily on the bay,
In your very own way,
A very sunny day.

Talula Purcell (8)
Anthony Roper Primary School, Eynsford

Roblox

There are millions of games
They are really fun
My favourite game is Tower Defence
My friends play with me
We have lots of fun
Roblox is my number one
Even my neighbours, Sophie and Luke play.

Thomas McMillan (7)
Anthony Roper Primary School, Eynsford

The Superhero Who Helps People

A special, superhero girl wanted to go to space to see aliens
And then when she saw an alien she was brave as a bear
Then when she saw the moon and the whole entire space she was excited
When she saw everything she was so happy
Even when she was a superhero she said,
"I'm going back to Earth because I'm a superhero, not an astronaut!"

Superhero, superhero, fly, fly, fly, superhero
Superhero, superhero, help, help, help, superhero
Superhero, flying in the sky
Up, up, high in the sky.

Santannamae Smith (7)
Barton Moss Community Primary School, Eccles

Astronaut Flying To Space

A stronaut flew to space in a rocket.
S trong rocket crashed and didn't break
T rillion people saw it on the news
R apidly more people saw it on the news
O n the news, people are shocked
N ame is Paul Cruse
A person on the news wants to try going to space
U nbelievably, now everyone saw him land
T onnes of people like Paul Cruse for one of the top ten records!

Logan Birkett (7)
Barton Moss Community Primary School, Eccles

Welcome To The World Of Nature

I am a human
I'm tired of cities
I'm going to nature
To find peace.

Long and shady trees
And that cool breeze
Made me relax and calm
And found the tree of palm.

The plain ground
With flora and fauna
And silence all over the area
Made me feel peace.

The clouds were as light as air
And blew the wind
And the sun set
Was the day's end.

Yousef Alkeshif (9)
Barton Moss Community Primary School, Eccles

The Man In Hell

The man was mysteriously walking and he was terrified of his unidentified land. Entering Hell, he was scared to go. His heart was beating fast as a demon went rapidly around him. Now he was terrified of this monster. In his soul, was fear.

Now he was running to the exit. His eyes in disbelief, he entered the universe. Someone whispered, "Liel, make me cry, saddle up Liel, make me fly up, up, away."

Joseph William (7)
Barton Moss Community Primary School, Eccles

Friendship

F un and laughter,
R espectful to each other,
I am kind to my friends.
E verybody plays together,
N obody is left behind.
D on't upset your friends.
S hare your sweets,
H ave lots of fun.
I love playing out with you,
P laying with my best friend in the whole wide world.

Logan Bell (7)
Barton Moss Community Primary School, Eccles

Autumn

Leaves go red, orange and gold,
I crunch through fallen leaves,
The smell of bonfires in the distance,
Smoke curls up into the sky,
Conkers fall from their spiky shells
And the leaves start to fall from the trees.
Pumpkins appear, faces carved into them.
Autumn feels like magic all around.

Poppy Farley Kirby (9)
Barton Moss Community Primary School, Eccles

Unicorn To Mars

Unicorn, unicorn, fly to Mars,
Unicorn, unicorn, make me fly.
Unicorn, unicorn, come and sing,
Unicorn, unicorn, come and play.
Come and make us fly,
Come on unicorn, let's play.
Unicorn, unicorn, for evermore,
Let's play like we have always done before.

Inioluwa Falusi (7)
Barton Moss Community Primary School, Eccles

The Shooting Star

The shooting star was soaring free in the sky
And someone was chasing it
It crashed into the moon
I found it and saw it wasn't shining anymore
Myself and my friends put tiny bulbs inside it
And launched it into the sky again
It was a triumph as it worked.

Jacob Taylor (9)
Barton Moss Community Primary School, Eccles

Witches Cry

Unicorn, unicorn make me fly.
Unicorn, unicorn make the witches cry.
Unicorn, unicorn make a pie,
Unicorn, unicorn make a cake.
Unicorn, unicorn make me fly,
Baffle the witches and make them cry.
Now get the universe to make them cry more.

Joseph Dean (8)
Barton Moss Community Primary School, Eccles

Nature To Happiness

Nature is adventurous
Lovely, has lots of activities, lots of fun
So colourful, really green and brown
Nature has crunchy leaves, really pretty and beautiful
Has pretty rocks that shine as bright as the sun,
and lots of trees.

Sophia Rosewhite (7)
Barton Moss Community Primary School, Eccles

Untitled

F antasy league
O ff-side
O pen net
T he cheering crowd
B all shoots towards goal
A player runs down the wing
L ines drawn half
L ionel Messi scores.

Christopher Oxton (7)
Barton Moss Community Primary School, Eccles

Unicorn To Space

Once a unicorn went to space,
Flying up up up up,
And then went to Mars
Flying from the galaxy,
For the unicorn, it was so fun
Galaxy, galaxy, so fun,
Galaxy, galaxy,
So amazing and twinkly.

Imogen Taylor (7)
Barton Moss Community Primary School, Eccles

The Suspicious Footballer

Footballer, footballer, score some goals
Footballer, footballer, win the Euro Cup
Footballer, footballer, fly beyond the units of football
Footballer, footballer, become the ultimate footballer.

Tiwatope Daniel (8)
Barton Moss Community Primary School, Eccles

The AstroBot Stuck In Space

Once upon a time, there was a bot stuck in space, navigating for help.
Rescue ships soon appeared but lost signal and crashed in shock.
One of the Astros survived on the mission to save everybody.

Greyson Atherton (7)
Barton Moss Community Primary School, Eccles

Things About Me

C orn is a nice food
O n-time sometimes
N ever mean
N athan is my best friend
O n my PS4 most of the time
R eally musical

Connor Swanson (7)
Barton Moss Community Primary School, Eccles

World War 2

People cheering,
As the soldiers are getting prepared,
For the war that is soon to come.
The children are being kidnapped.
People are running from the news.

Henry Willetts (10)
Barton Moss Community Primary School, Eccles

Friendship Time

E lephants are my mum's favourite animal
V ery kind is the way to be
I love playing around outside
E vening is the best time.

Evie-Leigh Evans (7)
Barton Moss Community Primary School, Eccles

World War 2

Lorries passing by,
Crying all night with my mum.
Dad at war all night,
Leaving in the day, bye, good night.
Getting nervous,
I'm scared.

Melissa da Silva Bavaroski (10)
Barton Moss Community Primary School, Eccles

World War II

Fighter jets go by
Children cheering they could win
Soldiers say it's fine
Explosions loud from afar
Parents screaming they're gonna die.

Charlie McCarthy Boyle (11)
Barton Moss Community Primary School, Eccles

World War Two

The war rushing by,
No safety in sight tonight,
There can be no peace,
And there's forgotten hope there,
Though we must take our time now.

Max Appleton (10)
Barton Moss Community Primary School, Eccles

Untitled

Deep tracks in the mud
Children screaming in the town
In the nick of time
Parents scared for their children
As loud booms bang in the night.

Dakota Baker (11)
Barton Moss Community Primary School, Eccles

World War Two

Tanks go to the war
Grinding the ice as they go
Soldiers looking sad
People are scared for their dear lives
Blackout windows hide the war.

Lylah Wells (10)
Barton Moss Community Primary School, Eccles

World War Two

There were guns and bombers,
Tanks devastating the town,
The planes flew to war,
Evacuees scared and sad,
The Luftwaffe circling high.

Sonny Macdonald-Boyd (10)
Barton Moss Community Primary School, Eccles

World War Two

Lorries grinded by.
Rose followed the lorry tracks.
People watching Rose.
She did not care who saw her.
Rose ran after the lorries.

Clara Swanson (10)
Barton Moss Community Primary School, Eccles

World War Two

Fighter jets fly by
German bombs dropping nearby
Fighter jets crashing
Soldiers shooting and running
Lots of soldiers passed away.

Jayden Sufyaan (10)
Barton Moss Community Primary School, Eccles

World War Two

Lorries grinding by
Deep tracks channelled in the mud
People standing near
Guns and bombs were everywhere
Evacuees safe and sound.

Dillon Shannon-Larkin (10)
Barton Moss Community Primary School, Eccles

World War Two

Ready to leave home
Bag packed and label on me
On the train I cry
Where will I sleep this evening?
Children in the back of vans.

Chloe Griffiths (10)
Barton Moss Community Primary School, Eccles

World Way Two

Lorries grinding by
Deep trucks stuck sadly in mud
People crowded near
As my mind fell to sadness
I wish the war were finished.

Abimael Remesha (10)
Barton Moss Community Primary School, Eccles

World War Two

She puts on my tie
And does up my top button.
I try not to cry,
Body trembling, so fearful,
I'm leaving at noon, goodbye.

Lindsay Umbaca (10)
Barton Moss Community Primary School, Eccles

World War Two

Bombers, grinding by
People standing, cold and sad
The war rushes by
Deep tracks channelled in the mud
When will the war end?

George Firth (10)
Barton Moss Community Primary School, Eccles

World War Two

People standing by
Deep tracks covered in wet mud
Fighter jets fly by
Bombing cities in The Blitz
As I leave London behind.

Krystal Wynter (11)
Barton Moss Community Primary School, Eccles

World War II

Waving flags up high
Saying goodbye to the men
Children screaming in the vans
My teary eyes watch in fear.

Scarlett Gilbert (10)
Barton Moss Community Primary School, Eccles

Stand Out And Be Different

It's a bit hard to fit in at school,
But if you don't you'll be cool!
Always be yourself no matter what.
If you don't fit in and look the same,
People will find you interesting.
Be positive even when you're feeling down,
Everyone around me are always in their crowds.
Sometimes they don't even listen when I talk out loud.
All the people in school,
Might not think you are cool.
Just because you're not fitting in,
Doesn't mean they treat you like a fool.

Lucia Sullivan (9)
Blythefield Primary School, Belfast

My Mummy Is The Best

My mummy is the best,
She never, ever rests,
She works hard every single day,
To make my future very bright,
She teaches me new things every day,
And there is always time to play,
She acts like a teacher to me,
That is why I am not afraid to be me,
One day, I will repay all her sacrifices,
I am proud that she is my mummy,
And I thank her every day for her love and care forever.

Hilton Gorman (9)
Blythefield Primary School, Belfast

My Friend

I shall walk with you,
To the ends of the Earth.
No more room to roam,
I will take you home.
When you stray and falter,
No more judgement will alter.
Our blood pact sworn,
In service of your ends,
My wish for you,
Oh dearest friend,
To find peace in this life,
Or what comes after.
My goal until there is no more room to roam.

Amelia Rea (10)
Blythefield Primary School, Belfast

When My Brother Smiled At Me

When I found out I was getting a baby brother,
I was sad.
When my baby brother was born,
I was sad.
Nine years of being an only child has ended.
When my baby brother smiled at me,
All my sadness disappeared.
When my baby brother smiled at me,
I was happy.

Kayleb Wightman (10)
Blythefield Primary School, Belfast

A Crazy Child

A small child runs by.
She has black hair, a red dress, scarlet lips, grey eyes
and black shoes.
She is stopped by a teacher.
Told off.
But guess what?
She bites her!
Blood oozes out.
Guess what?
She slurps it up.
No one moves.
She runs out, laughing.
Then, she flaps her arms and flies!
We are in shock.
What just happened?

I see her the next day on her own.
She looks like an angel.
Black hair sleek and tidy.
But, after yesterday, no one goes near her.
She screams.
Everyone stops what they are doing.
She runs to a boy named Jack and bites him!
She sucks his blood and flies off.

Never have I seen her again.
I am glad, too.

Zoë Appleyard (9)
Fawcett Primary School, Trumpington

The Sky

As the clouds go by
And the birds fly high
I wonder what's in the sky
Beyond the clouds
Where is the sky hiding
I need to know
When it pours it down
I give a frown
When it clears
Everyone cheers
The sky, the sky
What an amazing view
Maybe you could see the view too
If you look closely you may see
Flying aeroplanes going across the sea
When it is sunset
The sky starts to change colour
Making a sunset that you could share
With each other
When it turns dark
The sky says, "Night, night."
Wishing a good night to you all.

Lewis Jack Chesters (9)
Fawcett Primary School, Trumpington

Switch It Up

Swish swash switcheroo, you are me and I am you.
Swish swash switcheroo, you are me and I am you.
You are Halley, I am Malley.
You are Jacky, I am Mackey.
You are Sally, I am Dally.
Swish swash switcheroo, you are me and I am you.
You are Tracey, I am Casey.
You are Jerry, I am Perry.
You are Clair, I am Blair.
Swish swash switcheroo, you are me and I am you.

Akira Lyons (9)
Fawcett Primary School, Trumpington

Spring Blossoms

Blossoms tint the sky,
As petals drift, dreams will glide,
Soft blush in the light.
Sweet like butterflies,
A sign to show that spring has come,
Soft and delicate.

Lucy Zhang (9)
Fawcett Primary School, Trumpington

A Year Of Seasons

Spring, summer, autumn, winter; the four main seasons of the year.
As the seasons of the year may appear severe,
We may as well cheer for all the seasons of the year.

River Szabo (9)
Fawcett Primary School, Trumpington

Winter

Summer without family
Is like a poem about winter
Winter without family
Is even colder.

Lena Nikolic (9)
Fawcett Primary School, Trumpington

The Storm

Sometimes I feel anxious,
Sometimes I feel fine,
When those butterflies fill up my stomach,
It makes my eyes want to cry,
Feelings are strange things,
My heart desires to stay calm,
But when I conquer those fears
Wow, do I feel smart!
You are not alone with your feelings,
The rest of us get them too...
Not at the same time;
Nothing is straight like a line,
But together we all get through!

Emmie Mae Dalzell (9)
Greenways Primary Academy, Stockton Brook

Football, Football, Football

There are lots of different sports
But football is the best
It's more fun than baseball
And better than the rest.

Football is my favourite sport
What else can I say?
It can be a lot of fun
When you know how to play.

Even though we can't win every game
The coach wants us to have fun
It doesn't matter if we win or lose
Our team's still number one.

Jack Stokes (9)
Greenways Primary Academy, Stockton Brook

The Last Blossom Tree

Every day and every night, a blossom blooms
A pretty pink flower in a tree
As pretty as a magical moon
But only one can be found in this mystical forest

Behind da waterfall and in a cage
A blossom tree blossoms
Butterflies flutter in the cave
But in the tree, a portal opens
To a mysterious world

Every day and every night, a blossom blooms.

Myra Kumar (10)
Greenways Primary Academy, Stockton Brook

Dreams

As soon as you fall fast asleep,
You will feel it bubbling in your head,
The dream is coming,
Get ready!

Boom!
Crash!
Thump!

What is it?
Wizards? Witches?
Goblins? Gobbling their delicious midnight feast.
An imaginary world with dogs that can talk?
Or at your idol's colossal concert?
Are you in a race where you can run as fast as a cheetah?
Did you float up into the sky and fly?
Did you join a band and play the drums?

Boom!
Boom!
Boom!

Oh, there is a good dream incoming!
Whoosh!
You are now in a special world.
You are given a special wand.
Whatever you point at will turn into... slime!
Point, point, point! And poke, poke, poke!
The whole world is slime now
Apart from you,
You are now slime
Oh no, the slime monster
Wobble! Wobble!

Like jelly
And then...
... It's time
... To wake up.

Millie-Rae Francis (10)
Kingsbury Primary School, Tamworth

Wonderbell Chime

W orlds of the existing faerie groves
O ne is left that only one person knows
N ot one other person could ever go past
D efending the gates are masked figures, a high amount, something I'd call vast
E very blood moon, the gate will light up
R unning away, the figures act like pups
B ut child beware of the faerie moon orchid
E veryone in Wonderbell knows the punishment is morbid
L ate one midnight a child here came
L ucy Chime, the tree of all fame

C hild as she was, not born as a tree
H er instincts were to steal now she's paid her fee
I do believe as the only one with access to Wonderbell Chime
M ore people should now know about Lucy's terrible crime
E veryone should know about Wonderbell's fate, if you steal from a faerie the punishment is great.

Georgia Addison (9)
Kingsbury Primary School, Tamworth

Cotton Candy Clouds

Up in the sky, clouds fly,
Singing and dancing like a butterfly,
Melodies sung every day,
Never being bored - making every day
A better day.

Clouds as fluffy as snow lower the sky
Dancing on the ballroom clouds,
Never tiring, never failing.

They never vanish,
Always there, throughout the day in the sky,
Will never leave, never cry.

In the night, they will never die
Always there by my side.
Making everyone's day shine brighter than the sun,
Joyful songs will never die,
Like the clouds - ask them why?
They always smell like fruits,
Never rot,
Helping the world
Be the best it may be.

Jasmine (10)
Kingsbury Primary School, Tamworth

Bedroom

As you step inside my room,
You will see a pink explosion,
Pink teddy bears, about 1000 of them,
Bang!
No!
My model horse fell over,
Making a domino effect,
Fell as fast as a greyhound,
Smash!
My piggy bank!
Ten pounds was expensive!
I paid ten pounds for that.

Now, let's go to my older brother's room...
Whoa!
This is... a mess,
Pants on the floor,
Hey! He took my pink teddy,
Give it to me!
Back now!
Eww, there are cockroaches on the floor,
How revolting!
Oh yeah, his pet tarantula!
Brown, an Arizona.

Philippa Harrison (10)
Kingsbury Primary School, Tamworth

Ollie Watkins Aston Villa Footballer

O ver the line the ball goes in.
L ike a world champion.
L ike a shining star on the pitch.
I n Villa they win because of him.
E verywhere he goes he scores.

W hat are the chances Ollie becomes number one?
A ston Villa's number eleven.
T o win you need him on your team.
K nown as a striker.
I n Villa he's known as number one for making them win.
N o one from Blues can beat him.
S aturday he scores and the crowd goes wild.

Evelyn Stokes (9)
Kingsbury Primary School, Tamworth

We Are Free

Picture me in the tall, topped trees
Leaves swirling in the breeze
It's too late to return
I'm free, I'm free.

Picture me, tall as a tree
Crunching through the swirling leaves
Trust me when I say
I'm free, I'm free.

Picture me, leaping through the leaves
Twirling in the breeze
My voice echoes
I'm free, I'm free.

Picture me, wild as a leaf
The mountain trees towering over me
The Earth and I
We are free, we are free.

Jessica Hawkins (10)
Kingsbury Primary School, Tamworth

Friendship

F riendship is very good and important to people,
R elationships with very good friends,
I 'll help my friends at school.
E very time I go to school, my friends play with me in the playground.
N one of my friends are fake friends.
D ogs are my favourite friends to play with.
S chool is to help people make good friends.
H enry, my cat, is my friend.
I 'll help you make friends in school.
P eople love their real friends.

Summer-Marie Mari Dockerill (9)
Kingsbury Primary School, Tamworth

Friendship

F riendship is so important in life.
R eal friends are kind and helpful.
I have friends like you do.
E verybody has friends.
N obody should be a fake friend.
D ogs are my friend as well as people
S ummer is the best time to have fun with your friends.
H aving fun with my friends makes me feel happy, it might make you feel happy.
I 'm not a fake friend, I'm a real friend
P eople like their friends.

Scarlett Pardoe (10)
Kingsbury Primary School, Tamworth

Jhon Duran

J hon Durán always scores screamers,
H e never lets us down and puts up a fight.
O ver the goalkeeper, the ball goes in.
N obody can ever beat this mythical player.

D efenders go down with a scare and a fright,
U nable to stop him, he scores top bins.
R uns past the defender, scoring 1 or 2,
A s bright as fire, his eyes light up orange.
N obody can beat Villa's number 9.

Caiden-Jay Price-Butler (9)
Kingsbury Primary School, Tamworth

Bellingham

B ellingham is the best player in the world!
E arth is his home!
L earns more football skills every day!
L osing is not an option!
I s a very famous person in football!
N o one can defeat Jude Bellingham
G od bless Jude Bellingham, God bless him!
H e is always respectful to his opponents!
A s fast as a bullet he runs!
M y favourite football player by far!

Ali-James Djenad (10)
Kingsbury Primary School, Tamworth

Friendship

F riendship is key.
R emember you only live once.
I f you are kind, you will shine like a shooting star.
E njoy your loving life.
N ever give up.
D etermination, determination, determination.
S hine with your friends, enjoy with your friends.
H ope and love your friends.
I magine a world where everyone is friends.
P eace is better than arguing.

Layla Carnell (10)
Kingsbury Primary School, Tamworth

Halloween

H alloween, the spooky season!
A lone on Halloween night, might give you a fright
L anterns outside the house, shining like stars
L urking around in your street, asking for a treat
O ctober 31st, the day to trick or treat
W icked witches flying around at night
E ek!
E vil spirits sneaking around
N o jollyness in this season.

Jacob Blackwell (9)
Kingsbury Primary School, Tamworth

Sea Of Thieves

Sea of thieves,
We're heading up north,
As far as I can see,
As far as I want to be.

A pillaging pirate am I,
Taking lands across the sea,
As far as I can see,
As far as I want to be.

I am a rogue,
Not to be messed with,
As long as I'm alive,
I'll be on the sea,
As far as I can see,
As far as I want to be,
Sea of thieves.

George Abbott (10)
Kingsbury Primary School, Tamworth

Sunshine

The sun was a party hat
Bright, fun, orange
Dancing, dancing, dancing
Across the sky

The warmth felt like a blanket
A cuddle from the sky
Flaming fires fired forcibly
The star is a light bulb

Swish! Swoosh! Dazzle! Whoosh!
Sunsets like paint tins split across the sky
Pink, orange, red, yellow, purple
Kaleidoscope of colours.

Shelbie (10)
Kingsbury Primary School, Tamworth

Christmas

C hildren are so excited
H omes are being decorated
R ammed shops at this time of year
I 'm so delighted
S anta's coming to town
T he shimmering star on top of the tree
M istletoe hanging above me
A happy family celebrating next door
S anta please give me so much more.

Emmy Baker (9)
Kingsbury Primary School, Tamworth

Jude Bellingham

B ellingham is the best player.
E lectrifying, beating defenders.
L earning as he plays.
L osers don't stand a chance.
I nterferes with the fans.
N o one is better.
G oing to be the best.
H e is very kind.
A mazing, skilful and fast.
M an of the match.

Eddie (9)
Kingsbury Primary School, Tamworth

Imagination

In the starry night gloomy sky
There were clouds
Just as fluffy as cotton candy.
The stars, moon and clouds
Gathered in the misty sky
Like a group of friends.

In the day,
The sun shone,
As bright as a golden ring,
The boy's in royal blue
Sun
A ring of luck shining.
High above the clouds.

Evie Hope (10)
Kingsbury Primary School, Tamworth

Seasons

S un goes high, days get hot
E vergreen trees stay green in the wintertime
A utumn makes leaves go orange, gold and red as I walk through
S ummer skies shining blue
O ceans freeze when it is winter
N ight-time falls, and the next day falls
S pring is when the ocean melts.

Alfie De Paola (11)
Kingsbury Primary School, Tamworth

The Ocean

T idal waves swooping in
H appy people snorkelling
E ndangered species in the water

O versized whales doing flips
C rabs crawling on the coral
E lastic and plastic sadly in the ocean
A stonishing sounds of waves
N arwhals swimming blissfully together.

Felicity Green (10)
Kingsbury Primary School, Tamworth

Bubbles

B lue, white and rainbow-coloured, floating around
U sed to fly way up high
B ubbles are here for you to have fun
B lazing in the midday sun
L anding on the floor with a gigantic pop
E verybody loves to chase and catch them
S ometimes they fly way up high into the sky.

Myah Patel (9)
Kingsbury Primary School, Tamworth

The Sky

In the starry sky,
At night, shooting
Across the sky.

Stars filling up the sky,
Like the crowd at Villa Park.
Shooting stars shining,
Brighter than floodlights on historic nights.

We have to be there.

The ball shooting across the pitch like a comet
Across the midnight sky!

Ruby Benton (10)
Kingsbury Primary School, Tamworth

Spider-Man

S tringy webs come out of his wrists
P recious heart
I gnites his strength to save people
D ay after day, he saves people
E very day he goes on missions
R eally brave
-
M ighty cool suit
A s fast as a cheetah
N ever gives up.

Harley (9)
Kingsbury Primary School, Tamworth

Shih Tzu

Shampoo and conditioner every two months!
How do they run so quickly?
In the garden, running around and playing!
Tickling under their chins like cats!
Sleeping after running around, chill and calm!
Zooming all around, going mad
Under your bed all the time! Waiting for you to come in for the night!

Elin (9)
Kingsbury Primary School, Tamworth

Jude Bellingham

B est footballer
E ngland player
L ikes football
L oves being on the football pitch
I nteresting, amazing player
N ever gives up
G ood at football
H as talent
A confident player
M akes his team win matches.

Georgie Brooks (10)
Kingsbury Primary School, Tamworth

Lemmings

L ove is lemmings.
E pisodes are amazing and fun.
M ischief-making blue lemmings.
M y favourite character.
I s a cheeky bunch.
N aughty lemmings causing chaos.
G rizzy gets pranked by the lemmings.
S upercool tricksters.

Bradley Swan (9)
Kingsbury Primary School, Tamworth

Untitled

C uter than anything!
A n animal that loves to eat food
P urposely jumps on you
Y oung and silly like a clown
B angs on your legs with their head
A re very greedy
R ip and tear things easily
A sleepy, lazy creature.

Lacey Carruthers (9)
Kingsbury Primary School, Tamworth

Untitled

P eppers are my favourite snack
E very day I don't forget to pack
P aprika and Tajin spinkled on top
P acked with Vitamin C
E very piece freshly chopped
R ed, orange, yellow and green
S crumptious, juicy and super clean.

Lola Robinson-Stanley (10)
Kingsbury Primary School, Tamworth

Unicorns

U nicorns are so sweet
N ever to be found
I n fantastic, fluffy places
C uter than a dog
O n this fantastic land
R ainbows are their tails
N ever going to lose their sweetness
S o sweet! Never to be extinct!

Amelia Dunn (9)
Kingsbury Primary School, Tamworth

Jude Victor William Bellingham

B icycle king
E ngland midfielder
L ives for football
L ong shot specialist
I ntelligent
N o player better
G reat skills
H as speed
A mazing goals
M y favourite player

Freddie Vaughan (9)
Kingsbury Primary School, Tamworth

Werewolves

W icked howls of darkness.
E ngaged in hiding its victims.
R ips its enemies.
E nemies hide.
W alks violently.
O versized claws.
L eaps in the night.
F leeing in the night.

Tyler (10)
Kingsbury Primary School, Tamworth

Space

S un is a big star.
P luto is a dwarf planet.
A stronauts are people who have flown to the moon.
C annot breathe in space without a space suit and oxygen tank.
E arth is the planet with life.

Isaac Maloney (9)
Kingsbury Primary School, Tamworth

Football

F un to play,
O ff the pitch,
O n the pitch,
T o have fun,
B all flies like a shooting star,
A remarkable game,
L ove to play,
L ots of people's dreams.

James Charlton (10)
Kingsbury Primary School, Tamworth

Lion

L urks in the jungle and finds its meat
I nterferes with its prey so it can kill and feed
O n top of the jungle throne, it stands for the best
N o animal is braver than this, none like pests.

Alfie Barnett (9)
Kingsbury Primary School, Tamworth

Spectacular Sensational Space

Planets,
Beaming, lustrious,
Twinkling, gleaming, scintillating,
Stars, galaxies, asteroids, Northern Lights,
Brain-chilling, shivering, glistening,
Twirling colours, rotating,
Atmosphere

Sofia (10)
Kingsbury Primary School, Tamworth

Paradise And Inferno

Heaven
Radiant, elegant
Love, meaning and everlasting
Powerful, omega, Netherland, land of the dead
Torturing, tormenting, mind-turning
Hellish, underworld
Hell.

Rueben (11)
Kingsbury Primary School, Tamworth

Untitled

F un
O n and off
O n the pitch
T o be happy
B all
A memorable game
L ove the game
L ots of people dream.

Harvey Baker-Lewis (10)
Kingsbury Primary School, Tamworth

The Things That Happen When You Sleep

A diamante poem

Dreams
Unreality, fantasy
Floating, sleeping, drifting
Unicorns, rainbows, monsters, shadows
Haunting, horrifying, terrifying
Darkness, fearsome
Nightmares.

Isabella (10)
Kingsbury Primary School, Tamworth

Free Kick And Penalty

Green field, far shot
Initiating, shooting, breathing
Wembley Stadium, far shooting, close shooting, run-up
Retaking, faking, taking
White spot, close shot, penalty.

Billy Kinsey (10)
Kingsbury Primary School, Tamworth

Joy To Sadness

A diamante poem

Joyful
Effervescent, lighthearted,
Playing, laughing, loving
Excellent, rainbow, pathetic, tearful
Despairing, hurting, distressing
Cry, mourn
Sadness.

Kate (10)
Kingsbury Primary School, Tamworth

When The Sun Goes Down And The Moon Comes Up

A diamante poem

Sunlight
Golden, luminous
Shining, glowing, dazzling
Brightness, light, darkness, gloom
Glistening, glimmering, darkening
Pearly, silvery
Moonlight.

Sophia Henson (10)
Kingsbury Primary School, Tamworth

Seasonal Change

A diamante poem

Autumn,
Crispy, colourful,
Crunching, raining, falling,
Fog, ear-muffs, snowball, hot cocoa,
Sledging, ice skating, freezing,
Cosy, chilly,
Winter.

Alice (10)
Kingsbury Primary School, Tamworth

Yoda And Mandalorian

Baby Yoda
Verdant and tan coat
Eating, travelling, walking
Frogs, people, coffee, cat
Driving, finding, saving
Raven and silver helmet
Mandalorian.

Darcy-May Hollingsworth (10)
Kingsbury Primary School, Tamworth

Glistening Wonderfully

Sun
Shining, glistening
Orbiting, rotating, smiling
Midday, tucking into the clouds, hiding
Appearing, no light, glaring
Pouncing, wonderful
Moon.

Roxy Dovey (11)
Kingsbury Primary School, Tamworth

Football Poem

Aston Villa
Incredible, brilliant, winning, scoring.
Celebrating football.
North Holt End.
Missed goal, terrible result.
Horrible end to the game.

Jack Stewart (11)
Kingsbury Primary School, Tamworth

Pirates

A diamante poem

Pirates
Scary, terrifying
Sailing, roaming, exploring
Weapons, swords and cannonballs
Attacking, sailing, invading,
Sneaky, stealthy
Viking.

Bradley Smith (11)
Kingsbury Primary School, Tamworth

The Tale Of A Day

A diamante poem

Sunrise
Appealing, glistening
Shining, twinkling, rising
Sun down, moon up
Ombréing, darkening, resting
Outstanding, gorgeous
Sunset.

Olivia Holland (11)
Kingsbury Primary School, Tamworth

Emotions

Fear
Dark, scary
Terrifying, horrifying, terrorising thing
Smile, laugh, joyfulness
Heartwarming feelings, loving
Great, safe,
Happiness.

Millie (10)
Kingsbury Primary School, Tamworth

Life Cycle Of Kittens

Kittens
Small and fluffy
Playing, pouncing and eating
Fluff, fur, tail, long whiskers
Purring, hunting, sleeping
Unsociable, sleepy
Cats.

Bella (10)
Kingsbury Primary School, Tamworth

Witch

W icked women
  I nteresting objects in the cauldron
  T ricking children
  C ool, black cats helping them
  H appy cackling.

Ava (9)
Kingsbury Primary School, Tamworth

Aston Villa

Aston Villa
Best, great
Playing, training
Good, amazing, fabulous, brilliant
Kicking, dribbling, saving
Losing, winning
Birmingham City.

Mikey K-S (10)
Kingsbury Primary School, Tamworth

Cowboys And The Vikings

A diamante poem

Gun
Roaming, desert,
Riding, smoking, racing
Spinning, eating, fishing, fighting
Rowing, sailing, raiding,
Killing, singing,
Viking.

Connor Brunn (11)
Kingsbury Primary School, Tamworth

Sun And Moon

A diamante poem

Sun
Day, light
Blinding, lighting, heating
Space, galaxy, stars, moon
Illuminating, mesmerising, thrilling
Evening, dark
Night.

Poppy Dowdall Ford (10)
Kingsbury Primary School, Tamworth

Little Lamb

Lambs
Run around all gooey
Growing, playing, jumping
Milk, sheep, snow, fireplace
Snowing, raining, falling
Cold, frost
Winter.

Erin
Kingsbury Primary School, Tamworth

Snake And Spider

Slimy, scaly
Slithering and unlocking jaw
Wrapping prey, long, slimy wraps, twisting curves
Crawling, petrifying, climbing
Hairy, freaky.

Riley B (10)
Kingsbury Primary School, Tamworth

Cool And On Fire

Hot
Scorching, boiling
Holiday is decalescent
Warm, toasty, sweltering, burning
Freezing, chill
Icy, frozen, Arctic
Cold.

Annie (10)
Kingsbury Primary School, Tamworth

Seasons

A diamante poem

Summer
Fun, hot
Playing, laughing, tanning
Beach, sun, snow, clouds
Snowing, freezing, shivering
Cold, cloudy
Winter.

Chloe Spooner (11)
Kingsbury Primary School, Tamworth

Earth

E arth is amazing
A round the sun
R otates the sun
T aking 365 days
in **H** abited by life

Scarlett (9)
Kingsbury Primary School, Tamworth

Cats

C ats are intelligent.
A t lunchtime cats are excited.
T hey are happy when getting treats too.

Izaiyah Ashton (9)
Kingsbury Primary School, Tamworth

Imagination

Love is in the air,
And it is everywhere.
Love is touching ground,
From up and down.
It's fantastic,
So unelastic.
Full of imagination,
And wonderful anticipation.
Rainbow clouds and fifteen trees,
Pink and blue, purple and green.
Stars are bright,
And they sparkle at night.
All around galaxies asteroids in the air,
Hitting the moon in despair,
Holding light,
In the night.
Vampires and ghosts in my home,
All around guns get shot,
A lot.
Wonderverse filled in space portals round,
In my friend's faith round to the moon.
Me and my friend floating around in space,
Astronauts haven't even seen our face!

Jiya Palikondawar (9)
Oakridge Junior School, Basingstoke

Friendship Everywhere To Share

Friendship is a priceless gift
Which cannot be bought or sold
From the beginning to the end, friendship will still behold
True friends are as rare and precious as gold
Friendship is a beautiful garden, the more you put into it, the better it grows
From the moment, the same way that friendship does
When the sun rises and your friend is nearby
So be surprised when you rise from bed
So be impressed with all your friends.

Avana Rai (8)
Oakridge Junior School, Basingstoke

Never Will I Write Poetry

"No! No! No!" said Jimmy, "I won't write a poem. I refuse. I'd rather draw a truck and snooze."
I hate when Mrs Vinegar demands that I hold a pen in my hand.
Creative, I refuse to be.
I'd rather play or climb a tree.
Football plans are just the best.
Or chats with friends.
Or snooze or rest.
"No! No! No! I shan't. No! No! No! I can't write a poem. I'm not an old aunt!"

Samuel July (10)
Oakridge Junior School, Basingstoke

The Lion And The Mouse Comparison

The lion is powerful, the mouse is weak
The mouse is clever, the lion is dumb
But the lion and the mouse make a great combo
The lion is loud, the mouse is quiet
The mouse is sneaky, the lion is frank
But the lion and the mouse make a great combo
The lion is a carnivore, the mouse is an omnivore
The mouse is tiny, the lion is giant
But the lion and the mouse make a great combo.

Ankush Dhara (9)
Oakridge Junior School, Basingstoke

The Earth

The plants are dying
Trees being cut down
It doesn't help
It makes it worse
Smoking doesn't help either
Stop this with me
To make the world a better place
Stop people hunting down animals
Even the bees
Or we wouldn't be alive
Even killing bees gives us no food
Don't waste paper
Trees being cut down
To make paper.

Harris Snyder (8)
Oakridge Junior School, Basingstoke

Crystals

Crystals from the sky
Are quite sly
Falling to the ground
Not looking around
Not making a sound
Flat on the floor
Flat as a door
Thank you for listening
Stars are glistening
Up in space
With an untied shoelace
Dark stars connected
Looking like a shark
Crystals from the sky...

Tarunya Yakeshwaran (9)
Oakridge Junior School, Basingstoke

The Apple Forest

Once upon a time, I was walking through a forest,
And discovered there were apples on the trees,
And birds in the sky,
And a beautiful butterfly,
And a girl riding a bike with no one in sight.

So she was in for a fright
When it became night,
What a beautiful night sky.

Namaya Whitby (7)
Oakridge Junior School, Basingstoke

Life

Life is amazing, it is a fleeting breath of dawn
It dances on edges, frail and worn
Moments flicker, soft and bright, whispers in the silent night
Dreams collide with waking rays
In the spiral of our days
Hold each moment, big and true
Life is a canvas, coloured by you.

Gabriel Daniel (9)
Oakridge Junior School, Basingstoke

The Truth About Monsters

Monsters are strange, monsters are scary
Monsters are good and some are bad
Monsters have one eye and some don't
Monsters are great and some are kind
Monsters are heroes and some aren't
Monsters can rule the world
Or maybe not.

Greatness John (9)
Oakridge Junior School, Basingstoke

Music

The lovely lyrics light up my world,
The majestic melody makes me feel unstoppable
The deep dynamics develop me
To change my noise pitch
Music is wonderful worldwide
However, happy music makes me happier.

Cami Durham (10)
Oakridge Junior School, Basingstoke

Cherry Blossom Falls

Haiku poetry

Cherry blossom falls,
Pink petals, soft and mellow,
Fields lush and bright green.

Soft, silky flowers,
And dandelions yellow,
Easy to be seen.

Pastel summertime,
Gently floating slowly down,
Falling gracefully.

Daisy Pocock (9)
Oakridge Junior School, Basingstoke

Untitled

Three space heroes in space and all at once, not a single lost. Found aliens in the dark. All of them were scary. They were villains because they were evil and hidden very well and they were very dangerous.

Dunamis John (7)
Oakridge Junior School, Basingstoke

Jasmine And Freya

Jasmine and Freya met at a club.
Then every time they saw each other,
They would call her brother Stinky Sam
And laugh all the time.

Jasmine Jelf (7) & Freya
Oakridge Junior School, Basingstoke

All Year Round

Snowdrops bloom in the season of spring
Leaves emerge from the bare branches of the old oak
Leaving it with a blanket of cosy warmth.
Baby lambs thrive in their new habitat adapting perfectly
Like the last piece of a puzzle.

Sunflowers sprout in the season of summer
The leaves provide an intense moss green
Which smothers across the leaves like piles of money.
The sun is bold and bright
It bedazzles the sky with help from the sun rays
That guard the sky away from any darkness.

Leaves crisp in the season of autumn
Squirrels harvest their acorns
Leaves turn a fiery orange when summer passes
And the autumn blossoms
From the depths of the underground.

Frost freezes in the season of winter
Like a robber, the winter takes the leaves
And leaves it bare for the spring to repair

Snow danced down onto the musky street
Filled with devotion to cover the whole street
With a blanket of frosty ice.

Elula Manning (11)
Rushton Primary School, Rushton

The Awakening Of All Four

Winter, spring, summer, fall.
They are all the seasons, four in all.
Winter, frosty snow lays low,
The days are short, the nights are long.
Spring is near, let's move along.

Spring, flowers watch as their winter coats melt.
Field mice awaken from their sleepy slumber.
Lambs are born into an exciting wonder.
Summer is near, so let's move along.

Summer, cool waves roll off the bay.
The sun kisses my pale skin away.
Rays of light shine down bold and bright.
Fall is near, so let's move along.

Fall, red, orange, gold and brown.
Leaves scatter across the town.
Pumpkin picking from the patch,
Choose your favourite batch.

Nature's blanket covers the sky.
Prickly hedgehogs say goodbye,
On the late October night
Where they snuggle up nice and tight.

Sophia Holland (10)
Rushton Primary School, Rushton

Untitled

Milky Ways covering the universe
Stars burning like fireballs
Planets circling the sun

The air is frozen
There is no light
The planets are big, brave and bold

Gazing up, hearts filled with awe
The universe, without a flaw
In every star, a wonder raw
In space, our imaginations draw.

Fall, red, orange, gold and brown
Leaves scatter. across brown the town
Pumpkin picking from the patch
Choose your favourite batch
Nature's blanket covers the sky
Prickly hedgehogs say goodbye.
The late October night
When they snuggle up nice and tight.

Elsa Monk (10)
Rushton Primary School, Rushton

Our Earth While Growing Up

You don't know how quick time flies
But one minute you go from five to twenty-five
Four seasons in a year
Before you know it, it is time for Christmas cheer
Spring, beautiful blossoms bursting out of their little shell
Summer, while the daylight gets longer
You have time to get stronger
Autumn, as temperatures drop
You go to the shops
And get long-sleeved tops
Winter, heavy ice makes coats feel nice
This is the season for snow
Just enjoy every bit of life
Because it goes too quick.

Lawrie Adams-Knowles (11)
Rushton Primary School, Rushton

The Passing Of Seasons

Spring mild and sweet,
Petals delicate and neat.
By every flower you meet,
Comes a new life.

Summer toasty and warm,
Like a fresh baked pancake on a stove.
Dry lips becoming vibrant,
Just like an elderly conker alone.

Autumn crispy and nippy,
The sun running to hibernate.
Leaves sway back and forth to the floor,
As they crunch to the ground.

Winter like a blanket of white,
Invading the town of light.
Whipping wind smacks you,
Trying to give you a fright.

Amelia Scott (11)
Rushton Primary School, Rushton

Autumn Joy

Gleaming autumn leaves I've found,
Like golden flames in heaps on the ground,
As they try floating free,
The wind runs away, almost with me.

The sun settles, quiet and cold,
Like a frosted ember, proud and bold,
An orange glow, so warm and bright,
Retreats at the sight of darkness seeping into the night.

The acorn thieves sneak out at dawn,
Whilst the early workers stretch and yawn,
As winter comes near, that lonesome little leaf is now not gold
But brown, shrivelled and old.

Jaya Pooni (10)
Rushton Primary School, Rushton

Inner Harmony

It's okay not to be okay
Your mind will craft its own way
Give yourself a holiday
Let your problems flow away
Like a river on a gleaming autumn day

Let your mind burst with flowers
You have been working for hours and hours
Your mind has secret superpowers
Mental health is yours and ours

Inner harmony is at your bay
Not everything is a neat array
Let everything work its way
You are not alone in this world's display.

Sophia Burnside (10)
Rushton Primary School, Rushton

Lost In Space

The air is frosted
Devoid of life
The vast is daunting
An overwhelming might
Numerous planets
Unwavering waves
Reach for the stars
Stretch up high
Let the solar winds pass you by
Atop a planet a beautiful dome
To find a place that you can call home.

Martha Ambery (11)
Rushton Primary School, Rushton

Wonder

Wonder, I wonder what's really in the sky?
Wonder, when you do it you feel like you never die.
Wonder, I wonder what's happening tomorrow?
Wonder, tomorrow will there be any sorrow?
Wonder, I wonder are dragons really true?
Wonder, can cats go moo?
Wonder, I wonder what would happen if I did this?
Wonder, would there be anything to miss?
Wonder, I wonder what would happen if I did that?
Wonder, would I get a new hat?
Wonder, what would happen if life is still?
Wonder, could one move a windmill?
Wonder, I could wonder, wonder, wonder, wonder, wonder,
Wonder, wonder, wonder all day long, I could wonder
About plants, myths and legends, but those are all for
Another day.

Elyas Ladak (11)
St Jerome CE Bilingual School, Harrow

Them And Me

Our skin as dark as the night sky,
Our smile broad, but not sly.
Laughter making our foreheads crinkle,
But also making our eyes twinkle.
Our cotton wool curls fluffy and soft,
My bun's so high it reaches the loft!

Now to *them*,
I'd rate *them* two out of ten.
Their skin is as white as a cloud,
Their smile solemn and unproud.
Their forehead is always furrowed, I don't know why,
And *they* don't respond when I say, "Hi!"

Today at lunch *they* tripped me up,
And made me spill the water in my cup.
Everyone roared with laughter,
And I cried so much after.

The next day one of *them* got hurt,
And this time the teachers *didn't* make it worse.
They helped one of them! They aided that child!
But they didn't aid me! That's completely wild!

No, it's not.
My skin colour's cold, theirs is hot.

A week later we formed a group,
We call it 'The Black Troupe'.
Now everyone is seen as equal,
Ahh! I'm relaxing and slurping treacle!

Eliana Dotse (10)
St Jerome CE Bilingual School, Harrow

The Beauty Of Every Season

I wonder, are there more than four?
Autumn, winter, spring, summer
Each with a charm, each with a lore
Autumn's wind whispers,
While winter's cold gusts roar.

Spring brings bloom, vibrant and bright
Summers heat a radiant delight,
But what about monsoon, with its rain so deep
A season of clouds where the world seems to weep

Oh yes, the monsoon with its chilly embrace
Winds that dance wildly, a fast-paced race
Cold and rainy, the earth drinks it fills
A symphony of storms that gives nature a thrill.

Then comes the thunderstorm, fierce and bold
With heavy rains and winds that unfold
Lightning flashes, a brilliant display
Nature's own rhythm in a powerful ballet.

I wonder, are there more? The seasons entwine
With whispers of weather that elegantly combine.
Each brings its essence, a story to share
A tapestry of a moment, woven with care

So let us embrace every season's embrace
Each with its magic, its beauty, its grace
From autumn to thunderstorms, all play a part.
Nature's own wonder, a work of true art.

Aaradhya Butani (10)
St Jerome CE Bilingual School, Harrow

The Griffin

There I was, going to school,
A normal school day,
Or so I thought,
Something began to rustle in the hay,
I went to get a closer look
And my, what I saw!
A griffin, looking up at me
With a rather large paw,
My mother always said,
"How could they be real?
Ridiculous, stupid, out of their minds,"
But here was the proof they really were real,
Wow, amazing, incredible,
Then the griffin got up,
It started doing all sorts of tricks,
It acted like it was a pup,
I really wanted to see some more,
But I was already late for school,
Well, at least I had something to tell my friends,
And they might have thought I was rather cool.

Evangeline Penhale (9)
St Jerome CE Bilingual School, Harrow

Happiness

Happiness is...
My lovely family that I live with
The great smell of victory
The little birds singing
My life that I love
The bite of cake that melts in my mouth
The summer days when the smiles grow on our faces
Also the winter days when Santa Claus comes with
lovely presents for everyone in the world.

Happiness is...
The bright look of the sun
The day when I grow up
The time when I went to the beach
The time I had my first bite of a sundae!

Have a look around
What makes you happy?
Maybe books
Maybe writing
When you are happy
That time is precious
No one ruins your happiness.

Antonia Radu (10)
St Jerome CE Bilingual School, Harrow

Calmness Is...

The feeling soothed me
Calmness is, to me, the shades of red
Calmness symbolises heavenly peace.
Calmness sounds like a violin player,
Playing the calmest of violin music.
Calmness smells like my delicious sweets
Calmness tastes like margherita pizza.
Calmness is me in the usual UK
Calmness is no murder and war
There is nothing better than zero theft
For when there is, the peace, calmness
Always breaks, for then, the year of a comeback
Never restores the heavenly peace and calmness.
Calmness, the silence of peace
Calmness, the feeling that would suit the world.

Pranshu Patel (9)
St Jerome CE Bilingual School, Harrow

Wonder, I Wonder

I wonder, I wonder if unicorns are real
I wonder, I wonder if there really is a tooth fairy
I wonder, I wonder if Santa gives me presents
I wonder, I wonder if there are monsters under my bed
I wonder, I wonder if mermaids are real
But these were my infant wonders, now I wonder
I wonder, I wonder if I can pass this test
I wonder, I wonder if I'm cut out for this job
I wonder, I wonder if I can pay rent this month
I wonder, I wonder what happens if I disappoint the people I love most
I wonder, I wonder, why can't I go back to that fantasy wonder?

Esther Afari (10)
St Jerome CE Bilingual School, Harrow

Growing Up

I wonder if you realised
The last time you
Pretended to sleep to get
Carried home.

I wonder if you realised
The last time you were
Excited to go to school and see
Your friends to play family.

I wonder if you realised
The last time you always asked
For toys instead of the latest phone.

I wonder if you realised
The last time you created
A dance with your cousins to show your parents
For a sleepover.

I wonder, oh how I wonder
If you realised
All of that
You didn't, am I right?

Katalea Lusha (10)
St Jerome CE Bilingual School, Harrow

Imagination

The moment I shut my eyes, my life of imagination came out.
Cotton candy trees spread,
Dolphins swam,
The sea's water glowed.
The rain left,
The rainbow hung over my head.
It was my imagination,
I now knew this place by heart.
It was my imagination,
The birds sang,
The butterflies swooshed,
The bees buzzed,
The children giggled,
The dinosaurs roared,
The seafoam swished,
The sand swashed.
It was my imagination,
I now knew this place by heart,
My eyes opened.

Chloe Giorgi (10)
St Jerome CE Bilingual School, Harrow

Happiness

Happiness tastes like my favourite meals
Happiness smells like sweets and rain
Happiness sounds like nature and birds chirping
Happiness symbolises the world
Happiness is the colour of the rainbow
Happiness is being with my family and friends
Happiness feels like dancing on big, fluffy clouds
Happiness looks like pages full of wonder
Happiness is like a midnight dream
Happiness is like delicious chocolate, melting in my mouth
Happiness is like having a warm, bedtime bath with lots of bubbles.

Bronwen Taylor (9)
St Jerome CE Bilingual School, Harrow

Jaws' Flu

Listening to seagulls
Sounds like wow!
Everything, pelicans
You need to bow

Fishing for trout and sharks too
Jaws is coming down with the flu
Everything is next to you
Just wait for someone to say, "Boo!"

We write a poem with Jaws
Now, you have to have some laws
You aren't allowed to write
He isn't allowed to bite

For now Lane and Rain, they do rhyme
But This and That don't have a pint
A pint of seawater of course!

Zain Elfara (10)
St Jerome CE Bilingual School, Harrow

Candy Land

One yummy, tasty marshmallow
Tastes as smooth as playing two cellos

Flying through the air are three sprinkles
Be careful not to get four wrinkles!

Then go into the cellar
To the wonderful world of five Nutella.

To finally finish your cakes
Add six lucky little flakes

And seven sour lemon lollies
To make you a bit more jolly

Last, but not least, add eight scoops of strawberry
Icing and you're free to go blueberry slicing.

Eloise Kira Misra (8)
St Jerome CE Bilingual School, Harrow

Happiness Is...

Happiness is...
Waking up to birds singing
Going into my bed with raindrops tapping the window
Going for excursions with my family
Watching football with my dad
Watching Chelsea play
Spending time with my family
Laughing with my friends
Having a good football match
The feeling of life
Helping my parents
Happiness is in all of us
Happiness is everything
If you're sad, it's nothing
Happiness.

Clayton Taylor (9)
St Jerome CE Bilingual School, Harrow

Happiness

Happiness is the colour of indigo.
Happiness is the symbols of a rainbow.
Happiness is the sound like the ocean spring.
Happiness is the sweet sense of a bouquet.
Happiness is the taste of doughnuts.
Happiness is the happiest time of all.
Happiness makes our lives relaxed.
Happiness is hidden in wonder.
Happiness is a door of happy lands.
Happiness is a kingdom with happiness.
Happiness is a party with surprises.

Huda Alinzi (9)
St Jerome CE Bilingual School, Harrow

Happiness

Happiness smells like my favourite fruits: mangos and watermelon
Happiness tastes like my favourite dessert: warm waffles
Happiness symbolises joy to me
Happiness is the colour bright yellow
Happiness sounds like everyone laughing together
One thing that makes me happy is relaxing in a comfy chair and reading a book
What makes me really happy is spending time with my family
Happiness is the best way to feel.

Sara Jang (9)
St Jerome CE Bilingual School, Harrow

The Beach

Children, happy, playing, running, the
sea dancing in the night, sand
underneath my feet, but I am
one of many feet with sand
between their toes, moon-
light dancing on the
waves, partygoers
craving food, freshly
made, then again
the same routine
but less excite-
ment, people
less excited.
Again that
happens and
again, 'til
nothing
Is left.

Georgie Gilbert Farnan (9)
St Jerome CE Bilingual School, Harrow

Excitement

Run, run
What should I do?
My teacher's trying to catch up to me

But I can't stop
Too much energy
I'm going to get in so much trouble

I'm so scared

Run, run
Now my face is red
Now I'm slowing down

What's my mum going to say?

You know what? Don't think about it

Finally I stop

Excitement.

Zuzanna Pasternak (9)
St Jerome CE Bilingual School, Harrow

Happiness

Happiness is,
The page of an interesting book being flipped.
The words of the book being said in my head.
The scrumptious taste of great-smelling Chinese food.
The quiet lullabies being sung from my mum's room.

Happiness is,
The stream flowing down the mountain.
Scoring a goal in football.
The crunch of popcorn when I watch a movie.
Getting a win in my favourite game.

Vinicius Tonelli Alves (9)
St Jerome CE Bilingual School, Harrow

Wonder Animals

I wonder why there was an owl
That knew how to howl
It was not bright,
There was no light
That is how it feels in a towel
I wonder why there was a cat
That lived in a hat
It was not agile
But it was fragile
That is why it sits on a mat
I wonder why there was a frog,
That sat on a log
It was not rude
But it had an attitude
That is how you are in a bog.

Sima Alkam (10)
St Jerome CE Bilingual School, Harrow

The Beach

The second I stepped out of my car, I ran into the waves
I got soaked
I got drenched
I was at the beautiful beach
The graceful beach
The lovely beach
As I stopped my fun, I looked around
I saw the sand stuck to my feet
Clung to my feet
The seagulls gliding through the air
Elegantly gliding
Oh, how I miss the beach!
I wish this day would go on forever!

Phoebe Afzal (9)
St Jerome CE Bilingual School, Harrow

Wonderverse

W onderverse is a competition
O f writing poems freely.
N ever give up when you make mistakes.
D read can sneak up on you, but be strong
E ven if you don't have an idea.
R hymes are fun.
V erses can come.
E ven onomatopoeia.
R epetition is good.
S imiles are great.
E ven metaphors, too.

Ayra Gupta (9)
St Jerome CE Bilingual School, Harrow

I Wonder...

Do we really need to grow up?
We grow up as tall as trees and as cool as me!
They *stomp! Stomp! Stomp!* with their yeti feet
And their giant jumpers made with random colours
I wonder, I wonder...
Is growing up hard?
We get to drive big shiny cars
And earn money from a machine! Oh blimey
I wonder... I wonder if jobs are hard
Do they have to work hard?

Alessia Zgripcea (10)
St Jerome CE Bilingual School, Harrow

Life

Live your life, don't just exist
Be kind and gentle because life is a gift,
You will fall, you will get hurt,
But keep trying with all your might,
Let's all work together, help everyone in need,
Nature gives back for all our deeds,
Be grateful for every day and
Be helpful in every way,
Life is beautiful,
Let's do something meaningful.

Advik Dubey (7)
St Jerome CE Bilingual School, Harrow

Being Worried

Being worried sounds like crying.
Being worried feels like sea salt water in your eyes.
Being worried tastes spicy.
Being worried symbolises screams.
Being worried is listening to the cries of birds.
Being worried is crying under your bed.
Being worried is hearing your heartbeat.
Being worried is feeling the tears fall down your face.
Being worried tastes like eating spicy jalapeños.

Zaynah Abdirizak (9)
St Jerome CE Bilingual School, Harrow

Fields Of Green

Fields of green, Mother Nature,
A million trees planted forever.
Until saws and scissors, hammers and axes,
Destroy life beginning to emerge.
From mud, roots, lots of different backgrounds
Merge together to make wonderful,
Wonderful
Flowers, fields, jungles, trees for a million bees
Buzz through a million trees,
Looking to find the queen.

Lily Morsley (10)
St Jerome CE Bilingual School, Harrow

Cool Ice Cream

Hot, sunny day which makes me feel like a superhero
Ice cream, whenever I see ice cream, I get crazy
Sometimes I go closer and closer, look for the ice cream
And then I go crazy when I go closer
After that, I run
And put the delicious chocolate bubble gum and mango ice cream in my mouth
And gobble it up
Then I get brain freeze.

Vidhan Patel (9)
St Jerome CE Bilingual School, Harrow

Home Sweet Home

Cosy and warm,
Old and worn,
It feels like home, my very own.

Quiet and loud,
Standing proud,
It's my home, I'm not alone.

Full of laughter,
Sometimes darker,
It's my home, my family's own.

Sometimes comfy,
Sometimes grumpy,
It's my home, as I've shown.

Bethany Olewe (11)
St Jerome CE Bilingual School, Harrow

Roller Coasters

Roller coasters roll here and there,
Up and down and all around,
Doing curves and hanging upside down,
Looking at the giant town.

Once you're done,
You want to redo the fun,
Take another round,
Till pleasure is found.

But don't forget the best part...
Loop-de-loops, a work of art.

Akrish Singh (9)
St Jerome CE Bilingual School, Harrow

Happiness

Happiness is joy in your heart,
Happiness can be cuddling on your sofa
Watching a movie with popcorn.

Happiness is joy in your heart,
Sweets, cupcakes, gummies and buns.

Happiness is joy in your heart,
When the sky is blue and a
Rainbow comes out.

Happiness is joy in your heart.

Hannah Elisabeth Lopez Rohrmueller (9)
St Jerome CE Bilingual School, Harrow

The Beach

Big waves coming and hitting the rock
Birds singing on a sunny day
Fish dancing underwater
Dolphins racing with each other
People playing with a ball
Kids eating ice cream on a hot day
People swimming in gentle water
Ice cream vans singing their tune attract
People to come and buy ice creams.

Aksh Patel (9)
St Jerome CE Bilingual School, Harrow

Beach

Waves were crashing on the rocks with the beautiful sound of water
Waves were drifting towards the horizon
Seagulls flying and chirping all around, fighting for food
People diving, making that splashing sound
The waves increasing, bigger and bigger each time
Sandcastle being destroyed by the water.

David Oliveira (10)
St Jerome CE Bilingual School, Harrow

Happiness

Happiness smells like a bouquet of roses,
Its sweet smell blemishes my heart.
Happiness tastes like sugar popping in my mouth,
Just the sight of it makes me laugh.
Happiness makes me feel like dancing in the heavy rain,
Splashing with joy.
Happiness is the light of my life.

Avika Gupta (10)
St Jerome CE Bilingual School, Harrow

Happiness

Happiness is being well-fed
Happiness is the colour red
Happiness is at the beach
Happiness is the taste of peach
Happiness is a fire
Happiness makes inspire
Happiness is the deep blue ocean
Happiness is the best emotion.

Happiness is for us to share.

Caspian Nunn (9)
St Jerome CE Bilingual School, Harrow

Happiness

Happiness is the sound of trees swaying in the wind,
The sun on my face,
Playing football with my friends at home.
The sound of rain on the ground outside,
Wind blowing on my face,
That is what makes me happy.

Asher Wellington (10)
St Jerome CE Bilingual School, Harrow

Ocean

O ceans are big and could be small
C lear, fresh, salty water
E verybody swims in the oceans
A n outstanding sea creature too
N ever been in the ocean!

Jana Alhilal (10)
St Jerome CE Bilingual School, Harrow

Anger Is...

Anger lives down in his cage
He comes out when you rage.
He's big, he's red
You do not want to mess with him.
The only way to get him away
Is to take a break.

Antoni Plantowski (9)
St Jerome CE Bilingual School, Harrow

What Am I?

I have a bill,
It's shaped like a duck's,
And you're in luck,
Because I also have a beaver's tail.
I have otter's fur,
And the webbed feet of a bird.
I can close my ears when in need of a dive,
So when I get food it will help me to thrive.
They say I'm the king of the divers,
Ruler of the riverbank.
I lay eggs like your favourite feathered friends.
I swim with great elegance,
And I come from down under.
I have one last clue for you,
And that is...
I live in Australia.
Do you know what I am?

Answer: A platypus.

Tommy Richardson (11)
St Osmund's CE Middle School, Dorchester

Special Bond

In the garden of laughter, where memories bloom
I trust you with all my heart since I've been with you, since the womb
Remember the time we watched movies until midnight
Then we lay down and watched the sunrise, it was very bright.

Like two stars in the sky, we light up the night
Together, we shine, everything feels right
What makes a best friend? Laughter and cheer
Or a shoulder to cry on, always near.

You're the puzzle piece that fits just right
With you by my side, everything feels bright
Like leaves in the wind, we dance and sway
Together we laugh, come what may
In the book of secrets, you hold the key
With you, I'm brave, I can just be me.

When storms come rolling and skies turn grey
You're my rainbow, lighting the way
From silly jokes to whispers at night
Every shared giggle makes everything right.

With dreams in our pockets, we'll conquer the sky,
Side by side we'll learn to fly.
A true friend's a shield, in battles we fight,
Always there to cheer me day or night.

We laugh at the silliest things, it's true,
Like that time we tripped and fell in the goo!
You share my secrets, my hopes, my fears
With you, I can smile through all of life's tears.

Friendship's a gift wrapped in trust and cheer,
Together forever, my friend I hold dear.

Mya Thorne (10)
St Osmund's CE Middle School, Dorchester

My Land

My book fell to the floor,
I bent to pick it up.
But just when my hand touched the cover,
Its pages flapped open!
I tried to jump away,
But the book would not let me!
I was being sucked into the book!

Colours waved past me,
As I fell through the story.
I cried out, "Oh no!
There's an angry dragon, heading straight for those innocent elves."
As images flashed past.
"But wow! Was that a unicorn I just saw?"

Further and further I tumbled,
Spinning and twirling,
Until, at last, I reached the ground.

As my feet touched down,
The whole of the land appeared.
Beautiful, beautiful trees,

And luscious, green grass,
Rivers that flow through villages,
Home to excitable, friendly young brownies.

A group, nearby, whispered,
"She should fly to the moon, which is a door!
She doesn't belong here!"
Unexpectedly, I started rising!
It felt amazing!
I guessed the brownies had made me fly!

But just then,
The land wobbled!

Then I fell out of the book!
It turned out,
My dad had picked it up.

I will be back!

Louisa Graham (11)
St Osmund's CE Middle School, Dorchester

Starry Night Sky

Up, up high in the starry night sky
As high as the clouds
And as bright as the sun
Beaming down on Earth.
As wide as the Universe,
The stars twinkling
Like a thousand lights up in the sky
The galaxies, a million different shades.
Aliens on Mars, looking from below
As the moon went by as fast as a race car
But little did they know there was Earth down below.
Other life seeing everything as they do,
The silent night went by
Like any other night before
As the humans slept
And the aliens gazed up,
Never knowing any of them existed.

Imogen Spracklen (10)
St Osmund's CE Middle School, Dorchester

The Game

Win, lose or draw
It doesn't matter the score
As long as you're playing and having fun
Oh, look you've won
Pass with class
Catch to help win the match
Score and want more
You love netball
Be friendly on the court
Defend till the end
Find space and win the race
Jump high, stand tall
You love netball
All and all
Play with your heart
And do your part
Brilliant sport
That you play on the court.

Esmaya Richards (10)
St Osmund's CE Middle School, Dorchester

Super Verse

Space is cool, space is wide,
But have you ever wondered what's inside?
There might be cheese,
There might be ice,
There might be everything you like.

It might be super,
It might be cool,
Or maybe all the planets give tissues.

Whatever is there, I'm sure it's cool,
And maybe, just maybe, we can see too.

Like astronauts on the moon,
With a flag there too,
I want to be there,
Don't you?

Temiloluwa Adenigba (9)
St Osmund's CE Middle School, Dorchester

Me And My Friend

Me and my friend are always arguing.
Me and my friend are always fighting.
I wish it would stop.
I wish it would pop.
I wish it would walk away.

We've sorted it out.
Hurray. Hurray.
BFFs till the end.
Yay.

Me and my friend are always happy.
Yay, yay, yay.
Best friends forever.
And that is a promise.
BFFs forever and always.

Annabelle Biswell Harvey (10)
St Osmund's CE Middle School, Dorchester

Autumn

Autumn getting colder,
Frosty and chilly,
Dark mornings,
Warm, woolly hats,
Gloves and fluffy socks,
Crispy leaves everywhere,
All on the ground, deep down,
Green leaves
To yellow leaves,
Orange and red,
Autumn surrounding everyone,
Tuck up and snuggle
In your toasty bed,
And in the morning
You will see autumn
Frost everywhere.

Molly Hurford (10)
St Osmund's CE Middle School, Dorchester

Friends

F riends stick together
R ound every corner, they take an adventure together
I n the hardest times, friends stick together
E ven in the hardest times, friends are there
N othing can ever end good friendships
D ay by day, they will be your friend
S o make some friends that are kind and considerate.

Lilly Warren (10)
St Osmund's CE Middle School, Dorchester

Dolphin Poem

D olphin, you splash about all day in the sunshine
O ut and about, splashing all day long
L azing with your fish friends
P laying with your funny friends
H appily splashing around
I n and out, splashing about
k **N** ocking past sealife.

Poppy Norman (9)
St Osmund's CE Middle School, Dorchester

Empress Of Space

She wanders across the galaxy,
Treading carefully on the stars,
The Milky Way written in her soul,
Black holes are her scars.

Beauty is within her,
She is within beauty,
Protecting the planets is her life's duty,
She attracts wanderers like a siren to a sailor,
A flower to a bee.

Her skin, like the many craters of the moon,
Her light is much more than a golden hour gloom.

Eyes shady as the dark void of space
Her dress silky with edges of black lace

You now see, she gleams in every verse,
But make sure she doesn't catch you in her lifelong curse.

Niamh Lewis (10)
St Therese's Catholic Primary School, Sandsfields

The Wonderful Winter

Kids run outside, excited for the snow,
Hearing *crunch*, *crunch*, *crunch* as they go.

On Christmas Eve, it's so silent you can't hear a thing,
Not even a ping!
On Christmas morning, everyone is merry and bright,
But children are upset, as Christmas ends at night.

They all sit down to eat their home-made dinner,
Pulling Christmas crackers, but only one is a winner.

Sarena Hanford (10)
St Therese's Catholic Primary School, Sandsfields

Axolotl

A lways swimming around the sea.
e **X** cellent food hunter in the sea
O n the sea floor, you will see an axolotl swimming around
L ots of colours to see. Will you get a chance?
O n the sea floor, axolotl sneak quietly
T o see an axolotl, look deep in the sea
L et's see if it's easy to see an axolotl in the sea.

Arabella Lowe (10)
St Therese's Catholic Primary School, Sandsfields

The Humongous World War

You can hear the gunshots... *Bang!*
All the bombs, run in fear to the bomb shelter
Boom! as missiles from the plane up high in the sky
The screams of the soldiers in agony
The trenches are so dirty and wet
The hospital tent all that is good,
All that is warm and clean
Is all that I need.

Cameron O'Mahony (10)
St Therese's Catholic Primary School, Sandsfields

In The Jungle

A mazing creatures big and small
N oisy monkeys swing between the trees
I n the jungle, hear the tiger
M onkeys scream loud and proud
A nteater eats all the ants
L ong snakes slither
S cary bears roam the woods.

Noah Gibbs (10)
St Therese's Catholic Primary School, Sandsfields

The Woods

In the woods
There is a little
Village. At the
House, there are lots of
Animals, including a little
Mouse, and trees of all
Sizes, big and small,
Someone big and tall
Comes to the abandoned
Tree house.

Dorothea Boland (11)
St Therese's Catholic Primary School, Sandsfields

Beach

B rilliant views I can see
E ntering the beautiful sea
A nd lovely views high up into the sky
C an you feel the golden sand slipping through your hands?
H ow was your day at the beach?

West Mainwaring (10)
St Therese's Catholic Primary School, Sandsfields

Bakugo

B rave as a tiger
A ngry as an ox
K ind of crazy as a dog
U nlucky as a spider
G reedy as a dragon
O verpowered.

Camden Greenwood (10)
St Therese's Catholic Primary School, Sandsfields

YOUNG WRITERS INFORMATION

We hope you have enjoyed reading this book – and that you will continue to in the coming years.

If you're the parent or family member of an enthusiastic poet or story writer, do visit our website **www.youngwriters.co.uk/subscribe** and sign up to receive news, competitions, writing challenges and tips, activities and much, much more! There's lots to keep budding writers motivated!

If you would like to order further copies of this book, or any of our other titles, then please give us a call or order via your online account.

Young Writers
Remus House
Coltsfoot Drive
Peterborough
PE2 9BF
(01733) 890066
info@youngwriters.co.uk

Join in the conversation!
Tips, news, giveaways and much more!

 YoungWritersUK   YoungWritersCW

 youngwriterscw   youngwriterscw